Positive Affirmations

ALEXIA EDEN

Author photograph: Renata Subic Photography

Interior design & typesetting: Alexia Eden

ISBN: 9798852449047

CONTENTS

-INTRODUCTION-

*T*his is a short collection of Positive Affirmations designed to imbue your mind with Positivity, Encouragement and Love.

These affirmations were originally presented on a YouTube channel, which I since took down. A couple of other creators re-posted them on their own channels, which turned out to be a blessing in disguise as they received such a positive response, that I decided to re-gather my own work here and re-publish it as a book! Everything happens for a reason! I trust that whoever finds this book helpful will be guided to come across it.

Please use these affirmations however best works for you- reading them, speaking them aloud, writing them out in a journal, mixing and matching them etc. You can also adjust any affirmation to your liking, inserting substitute words for example- if "the Universe" doesn't work for you, replace it with something that feels good to you, e.g. "Subconscious Mind, Higher Self, God, Source, Angels, Divine Source etc." I personally like to use Higher Self, Soul or Universe.

How to Use these Affirmations:

There are a lot of affirmations here; most are repetitive and similarly-themed to one another. You will probably be attracted to different affirmations on different days; it's fine to switch affirmations; just go to the ones you are drawn to at the time. Your intuition is your best guide in this life. Your intuition comes from your Soul, which always knows exactly what you need at the perfect time and knows the Highest Plan for you. You will always be drawn to subconsciously the right affirmations you need to elevate your vibration at the time.

Really, the goal isn't the words of the affirmation itself but the energy it creates and inspires within you. It is the energy we are aiming to embody. Go through, dwell on and repeat the affirmations you are drawn to till you feel a buzzing, excited/joyful or light feeling around you, inside you and through you. You will know when your energy has shifted. You only have to do the affirmations/feel the energy till you feel "saturated"- there will be a point where you naturally feel inclined to stop and happily get on with your day. It is like a "that's amazing, it's enough" and then you leave it and get on with your day happily. If you do affirmations daily like this, you will begin to naturally change your energetic setpoint. When your energetic setpoint (dominant vibration) is higher, you will naturally begin to attract more positive things and this will make it easier and easier to attract more good into your life, keeping the momentum going!

Stay positive! In the beginning, the only sign you may have that things are changing is that you gradually start to feel better, bit by bit. Often with manifestation, it looks like nothing is happening, and then there is a tipping point where all your unseen energetic shifts add up and overflow and manifestations pour or pop into your reality bit by bit into your life. Keep positive, have Fun with the process and be Optimistic! Expect Good things.

Final caveat: It is fine not to be Positive 100% of the time. Love (Divine Love/God/Source) doesn't need us to be perfect to love us. The more you go through the ups and downs of life, the more you will notice Grace and miracles are always there for you, through the darkest hours aswell as in the light. Even when it doesn't look like it, the Light is there.

Every single human on Earth has doubts, fears, worries, anxieties and bad days, because that is what it means to be human, otherwise we would be God! Although we are a part of God (the Universe/Source) and one with It, we are still human so do not beat yourself up for not being perfect. There is no such thing. If God wanted us to be perfect, he/she/It would have made us that way. Paradoxically, <u>with</u> all our vulnerabilities and flaws, we are perfect in God's eyes. Source made us imperfect so there is space and invitation for it to sweep us off our feet, or simply step in and quietly help us when we cannot help ourselves. The Universe loves to surprise and delight us, be there for us, comfort us and always be there guiding us at every step of the way, even when it doesn't look like it. Divine Orchestration is always at play behind the scenes. We are in a divine, loving, <u>Co</u>-creative Cosmic dance with Life. Stay positive as much as you can, and know at the same time that it's safe for you to trip up from time to time, because Life is always here for you. Everything is always, always working out for you, for your Highest Good.

1.

-POSITIVE MINDSET-

AFFIRMATIONS FOR POSITIVITY

*H*ere are some Positive Affirmations for thinking positive thoughts and changing your mindset to one of Positivity. What we think about, feel and vibrate at, we attract, so think good thoughts as often as possible and good will come back to you. The more good you give out, the more good you get back!

It doesn't matter if you have negative thoughts, for as long as the scale is tipped more dominantly towards the Positive, the Positive will take over in your life. Also note that Positive thoughts are much stronger than negative ones. They have more vibrational Power and gravitas, therefore if you think positive thoughts some of the time, the Positive energy will begin to spiral upwards and you will attract more good back to you.

Keep practising! Like attracts like; the more you practise thinking positive thoughts, the more they will begin to dominate in your consciousness and it will become easier and easier. **Positivity really is a choice**- you can choose to either be positive or negative.

When we are positive, we attract better and all good things into our lives, and **most importantly, being Positive Feels Good!** Choose Positivity, and you will soon see it is a far better way to live.

-AFFIRMATIONS FOR POSITIVITY-

- I only ever think positive, helpful, uplifting encouraging thoughts.

- My inner self talk is uplifting and joyful.

- I am my own best friend.

- I am my own cheerleader.

- I love and believe in myself.

- I am always there for myself.

- I am the Best.

- My inner self talk is that of a Winner.

- I love myself and I only ever see the Good in life.

- I think positive, helpful, loving, encouraging, uplifting thoughts about myself.

- I think positive, helpful, loving, encouraging heart-based thoughts about others.

- Love and Positivity fill my life.

- Love, positivity and laughter fill my life.

- I am always seeing the Positive in Life.

-POSITIVE MINDSET-

- I feel so lucky and blessed.

- I dwell on how fortunate I am and how lucky I am to be me.

- I love myself. Every day I wake up counting my blessings.

- I love myself. Every day I wake up and think how lucky I am to be alive!

- I turn every so-called "setback" that happens to me into an opportunity.

- I am lucky and positive.

- I am magical and Fire.

- I am optimistic, lucky, resilient and a Winner.

- I am full of Good Fortune.

- Life loves me.

- Life loves and works with me to fulfill my dreams.

- I am always riding the wings of Fortune.

- I radiate luck, Positivity & Good Energy.

- I radiate good Luck, Blessings and Opportunity.

- I am exciting, uplifting and electric to be around.

- Everyone loves me. I love myself

- I am uplifting and Positive.

Positive Affirmations

- I see the world through eyes of Gratitude and Love.

- Every day I count my blessings.

- I see the world through eyes of opportunity, luck and adventure.

- I am a risk-taker.

- I always see the Good in everything.

- Even when I lose, I win.

- Everything always works out in my favor.

- I radiate Positive, Loving Energy.

- I am Love, Magic, Fire and Bliss.

- I am a whirlwind of Love, Positivity, Luck and Magic.

- I radiate perfect Health, Beauty, Abundance and Joy. I radiate Gratitude and Love for the Universe

- My life is truly blessed.

- I am blessed.

- I am Positive.

- Everything always works out for me.

- I love Life.

- Life is on my side.

-POSITIVE MINDSET-

2.

-LUCKY, RECEIVING AND OPEN TO ALL GOOD -

AFFIRMATIONS FOR BLESSINGS

*S*imilar to the first chapter of affirmations, these are some Positive Affirmations to get you into the feeling of Positivity. This chapter is more based on *receiving* positivity, luck and blessings rather than *being* a positive person and giving it out.

Affirm your luck, blessings and good coming to you and this is what will materialize in your world!

We are all beloved children of the Universe. You do not have to do anything in order to receive from the Universe. You are worthy and deserving just because you *Are.*

You are the receiver. When you realize the limitless Power of the Universe and the endless depths of its love for you, you will feel naturally relaxed to receive.

Sometimes when we receive something, we feel obligated to give back, either to the person who gave the thing to us directly or out into the Universe so that we are giving and participating in an equal "energy exchange." We think that we have to give or do to be worthy of receiving, and that we cannot receive something for nothing. This is not strictly true. The person who is giving you something– whether it is money or anything else– is giving to you because you *already* gave them value. Whether it was a piece of work you did for them, your services or even just your presence, they already feel they received value from you so they are giving something to you to thank you and equate the energy balance exchange in their mind. Also, if this is something that has come from the Universe directly, e.g. finding money on the floor, you do not need to give it away the next day immediately for karma. The Universe gave you that money or gift as a token of its love and affection for you because it benefits from your existence– you are its beloved Creation. There are no strings attached.

Giving out of obligation, or because you feel you have to, is not a clean energy exchange. When you work on your receiving channels and allow yourself to become a divine conduit for blessings, there will be natural points where you truly feel an inspiration and urge to give!! When you follow these urges, you will feel joyful and loving and your recipient will also feel that energy. It is a win-win! Take care of your own receiving, and the giving part of the equation will naturally take care of itself.

-AFFIRMATIONS FOR RECEIVING-

- I radiate love and positivity.

- I radiate good energy.

- I am a powerful magnet for all good.

- I am a magnet for luck, good fortune and blessings.

- I am a magnet for love and respect.

- I am a magnet for appreciation and admiration.

- I am a magnet for success and abundance.

- I am a magnet for wealth and prosperity.

- I am a magnet for happiness and fulfillment.

- I am a magnet for love and romance.

- I am a magnet for perfect health and happiness.

- I am a magnet for confidence and beauty.

- I am a magnet for positive surprises.

- I have endless good luck and fortune.

- I am a magnet for lottery blessings.

- It feels so good to be a lucky money magnet.

-LUCKY, RECEIVING AND OPEN TO ALL GOOD –

- Money comes to me from exciting, unexpected delightful sources.

- I win money all the time.

- Lucky grand windfalls of money are pouring into my life.

- Good fortune befalls me now and forever.

- I am a magnet for lucky events, people, places and circumstances.

- Amazing opportunities come my way every day.

- I am always in the perfect place at the perfect time.

- The most loving, helpful positive people fill my life.

- Things always magically work out for me.

- Things always work out in my favor.

- Things always work out for me in the most magical and beautiful way.

- Everything is falling into place as planned.

- My destiny is better than I ever imagined.

- Life has a beautiful grand divine plan for me.

- Everything always turns out better than I ever imagined.

- Life unfolds in the most magical serendipitous way for me.

Positive Affirmations

- The Universe always brings me everything I desire and so much more.

- The Universe loves to surprise me and delight me with gifts.

- My life is full of wonderful surprises, love and blessings.

- I receive all good.

- I always receive more than I ever thought was possible.

- I am incredibly blessed by the Universe.

- Life brings me only the best.

- I deserve the best and I only attract the best.

- Life loves me. Life adores me.

- I am so grateful to the Universe.

- I am cocooned in the loving energy of the Universe.

- Life supports me. The Universe supports me.

- I experience love wherever I go.

- Love surrounds me wherever I go.

- The most incredible loving people fill my life.

- Only good comes to me now.

- Only good lies before me.

-LUCKY, RECEIVING AND OPEN TO ALL GOOD –

- I am open and receptive to all the good and abundance in the Universe.

- It feels so good to receive.

- I am receiving. I am receiving now. I am receiving all the Good and Abundance in the Universe now.

- I am open and magnetic to all good.

- I am open to the wonders of the Universe.

- I am open to the blessings of the Universe.

- I am open to the mystery and wonders of Life.

- Amazing things are happening for me now.

- The most wondrous over the top miracles happen for me right now.

- The most wondrous over the top miracles are happening for me this very minute/second.

- I am so happy.

- My Life always goes from strength to strength.

- I always move from success to success.

- Life always gets better and better all the time for me.

- My life is always so incredibly rich, abundant and fulfilling.

- I live an exciting, adventurous life.

Positive Affirmations

- I live at the peak of existence.

- I am at one with the Universe.

-LUCKY, RECEIVING AND OPEN TO ALL GOOD –

3.

-MONEY MAGNET-

AFFIRMATIONS FOR MONEY

*M*oney is a force of Love and Good in the world. Money is simply energy – a form of energy that the Universe uses to demonstrate its love for you! Money flows through people but it comes *from* the Universe. As we live in a loving Universe, that can only mean that the Universe wants to use money to bless you. Money can only be blocked by our wrongful negative thinking about it, therefore if we change or eliminate any negative beliefs and shape them into new positive ones, we begin to allow the Flow of money into our lives.

Money is a force of Love and Good and can be used to bless and prosper others, connect with others, share and receive, expand our experiences and support us to live in comfort, beauty and joy. We can do a lot of good with money and use it as a tool of light. You can never help anyone from an impoverished place- you may be able to help someone despite being in an impoverished place, but never because of it. You will always be able to do more good with money than without it.

Money manifests in our realities in accordance to the beliefs we are holding about it, so let's make sure they are positive, empowering ones- beliefs that unblock the floodgates and allow the money to flood in!

-AFFIRMATIONS FOR MONEY-

- I am an absolute magnet for money!

- Money loves me. Money loves to support me and show up everywhere for me

- Money is a demonstration of the Universe's love for me. Money is the Love of the Universe in action

- I adore money and money adores me!!

- I am in a loving, healthy, exuberant relationship with Life, and Money!

- Money loves me! Money adores me. Money is my best friend.

- Money just loves to be around me.

- I love and respect money and all it does for me. I respect and love my money and treat it well.

- I have the healthiest, most fun, loving nourishing relationship with money.

- My wallet/purse is always stuffed full of cash

- Money loves to surprise me in the most delightful, unexpected ways!

- Money is a loving, supportive energy from the Universe. I let the love of the Universe in

-MONEY MAGNET-

- I accept my worthiness. I am a beloved child of a Loving Universe and I deserve to receive

- More and more money is pouring into my life

- Money is compounding, overflowing and extravagantly present in abundance in my life

- I always have more money than I know what to do with!!

- Money constantly flows into my life from the most amazing delightful sources.

- I am constantly receiving such jaw-dropping amounts of gorgeous money and it all comes from the most exciting, fulfilling integrous sources.

- I only ever receive money in ways that make me happy.

- I only ever receive money in ways that benefit all involved.

- I receive mountains and avalanches of money in abundance constantly.

- I am just a complete magnet for money

- Avalanches upon avalanches of income are just pouring and pouring into my life.

- I only ever earn money in ways that make me happy

- My multiple bank accounts overflow with riches and excess.

- My purse is always stuffed full of endless wads of cash.

Positive Affirmations

- Why is so much money always pouring into my life?!

- I am so lucky, generous and blessed!

- I love to give and share and receive. I only ever give in ways that feel good and joyous to me.

- I deserve my abundance

- I accept money as a reflection of the Universe's utmost support, love and devotion to me

- I am completely free, wealthy, abundant and happy.

- It feels so good to be abundant, rich, financially independent, secure and fulfilled.

- I always easily afford anything I want.

- I love treating myself to the best of the best. Money is no object for me.

- I love splurging on myself and showing myself self-care using my money. I trust that there is always more where that came from!!

- I love treating my family, friends and loved ones.

- I always have enough. Way more than enough

- My abundance is endless and ever-increasing

- I live in an infinite sea of prosperity and wealth

- Life only ever gets better and better for me. I move into unlimited prosperity, wealth and fun

- I am always safe in the Universe

- I donate generously and lovingly to the causes I feel good about

- I give as much as I feel called to! The Universe protects me. I always receive back what I give out 2-3x back over.

- I have avalanches upon avalanches of savings and investments.

- My family and friends are so proud of me. They admire my financial success and independence and are happy for me.

- I am abundant, rich and free.

- I am financially independent, abundant, secure and joyful.

- I am abundantly, wildly successful, rich and happy.

- Every dollar I circulate always comes back to me a tenfold.

- I always find money in the street.

- I find shiny beautiful new coins of all denominations in the street.

- I find new beautiful crisp money notes of all denominations in the street.

- My life is like a video game. I walk around and I see shiny coins like treasure and beautiful crisp money notes glinting at me everywhere I go. All this treasure is embedded for me in my environment for the taking.

- People love to pay me for my services.

- People love to give me money!

- I always get tremendous discounts on what I want all the time.

- Everything I want always goes on massive sale whenever I want it!?

- I am the recipient of lucky money miracles all the time!

- Why does money love me so much!?

- Why am I always surrounded by wealth?

- Why am I so wealthy, abundant and happy!?

- People love to pay for my drinks!

- The baristas love to give me my coffee for free!

- People love to buy my coffee for me.

- Bartenders love to give me free drinks!

- People love treating me to lunch/breakfast/dinner all the time.

- It gives people great happiness to treat me.

- Every time someone gives me money or spends on me, they receive it back 10x over from a source that benefits all involved.

- Every time I help somebody financially or spend money on someone, I receive the amount back 10x over from a source that benefits all involved.

- I receive unexpected gifts all the time and I am delighted.

- I always receive extra at work!?

- My happy clients give me extra because they adore me.

- I get massive generous tips from wealthy customers/clients.

- I receive massive eye-watering bonuses at work. I am so incredibly valued!

- I am a magnet for wealthy clients who greatly appreciate me and love to reward me for my work.

- I always receive multiple amazing top job offers at a time.

- I always get salary raises and massive promotions all the time.

- I am always promoted at work and I love it!

- I always win competitions- the top amazing highest value jackpot prizes.

- I always win the lucky scratch-offs!! I am always cashing in on my scratch-offs.

- How am I so lucky with scratch-offs!?

- I always get the winning scratch-offs.

- I am a multi-time jackpot lottery winner!

Positive Affirmations

- I win the lottery and it feels so good.

- I win multiple lotteries, multiple times and grand prizes too!

- It feels so good to win the lottery. I am so lucky and blessed in life.

- I am such a winner in Life.

- I am a genius investor and I always pick the top-performing stocks/winners/coins.

- I am a genius, intuitive investor. I am a legendary trader

- I am so good at trading.

- I take great pleasure in investing because I always have more than enough capital to do so.

- Everything I invest always comes back to me minimum 10x over within just 5 years.

- I am the King/Queen of Money.

-MONEY MAGNET-

4.

-WEALTH AND SUCCESS DOING WHAT YOU LOVE -

AFFIRMATIONS FOR SUCCESS

You *can* have it <u>all</u>.

Most of us at some point in life, maybe several times, have traded off career and finances for emotional fulfillment and happiness. However, what if the truth is that we could have it *all*? Success AND happiness, doing what we love, where we want to live and who we want to be with? Living in comfort, joy, love, abundance, success, wealth and happiness....freedom doing what you love along with joy and success in your chosen fields?

It is an old, outdated and negative belief that we must work hard at a job we hate in order to survive. This idea is a hangover from previous generations where physical life was very hard. People worked in the fields and farms all day from dusk till dawn, before intense machinery. There was no technology, no internet, no telephones, no fast food (please note I don't advocate fast food unless it's healthy, but it's just an example of how everything used to be very slow and without modern conveniences we enjoy today!). This belief is still around and prevalent in society because so many people are still subscribed to it. However, you only need to buy into and consider a new belief - that you are worthy and deserving of happiness and that you can be, and are even *meant to* be successful, wealthy and happy by doing what you love! This means working at jobs, careers or businesses [for entrepreneurs] we love, working smart and not hard, being in the Flow state and loving our work so much that it doesn't even feel like work! A life where work is play and where the joy you feel in your career overflows into your entire life....your work-life enhances your personal life.

The more people believe this and manifest it for themselves, the more the collective belief grows more powerful and we create a better world! Your success is not selfish. Your success and joy doing what you love encourages and shows others that they can do the same! When you turn on your own light, you give others permission to do the same.

We are *meant* to do what we love. The Universe planted our divine wishes and desires in our hearts for a reason; we are all unique facets of the Universe expressing itself therefore when you pursue your dreams and desires, you are an aspect of the Universe creatively expressing and expanding itself. The only reason it appears to not be true is if we bought into the opposite; that we have to do what we hate in order to survive or make money. The Universe loves you enough to follow and manifest what you give it. It is only a false, outdated negative belief and the Universe will happily and easily manifest an empowering, new, helpful, more uplifting one for you just as easily as it manifested the old- when you are willing to drop your limitations and change your Consciousness.

The more you practise feeling the vibrations of Success, Happiness, Joy and Worthiness doing what you love, the more you will see it begin to manifest as your reality. Your belief will become stronger, life will become easier and easier and the more you believe it, the more you will see it! Crowd out your subconscious with feelings of Success, Love, Happiness, Worthiness and Fulfillment till it is overflowing with love and positivity, feelings of success and bliss. Feel the peace and quiet inner joy of knowing you are free to live the life you love, doing what you love, on your own path and watch it manifest as your life.

-AFFIRMATIONS FOR WEALTH & SUCCESS-

- I am incredibly successful

- My success is divine.

- My success was always meant to be.

- I am successful, abundant and fulfilled in ALL areas of life.

- My success, abundance and joy are overflowing.

- I AM pure success, pure happiness and pure bliss.

- I radiate fulfillment and expansion.

- I radiate the fulfillment of my dreams and desires.

- I AM pure success and pure fulfillment.

- My success always comes to me in the best, most delightful ways!

- My success is the BEST success.

- I feel so good about myself.

- I am so proud of myself.

- I believe in myself.

- I am an exceptional individual.

Positive Affirmations

- *I* am extraordinary

- I am a top 5% er

- I have my dream job/career/entrepreneurial business and I love it!

- I live my wildest dreams and am incredibly highly rewarded for it!

- I always get paid a fortune to do what I absolutely LOVE.

- I always receive a fortune to do what I absolutely LOVE.

- I work with the best, most amazing, incredible fun people who adore me!

- I am so incredibly loved and adored.

- I am so highly respected, appreciated and sought-after.

- I am a leader, top 5% in my industry.

- I am so looked up to and admired.

- I am highly valued and always in super demand in my industry.

- The very best people in my industry want to work with me.

- I am the most highly-demanded, top 5/best in my field.

- I add immense, enormous, priceless tremendous value to other people's lives.

- I have a unique, Starry presence that uplifts the planet.

- It is divine destiny to fulfill my heart's desires.

- It is the divine calling to fulfill the longings of my heart.

- My Success is destined.

- My success is assured.

- I now receive mountains upon mountains of money for being myself for eternity!

- I am myself and am incredibly rewarded for it

- I am so happy and fulfilled in life!

- It feels so good to get paid a fortune just for being myself!

- I constantly receive such high, vast amounts of money for being myself

- I always get paid a fortune to do I love

- I always get paid a montón to do what lights me up in every way.

- The Universe pays me to do what I love!

- The universe lovingly supports me in being myself.

- I am delighted that I live the life of my dreams and am abundantly supported in doing so

- I am delighted that I live my dream life and am highly rewarded to do so.

Positive Affirmations

- The Universe wants me to succeed even more than I do!

- The Universe wants me to have all my heart's desires.

- The Universe wants me to have it all.

- All of my deepest, wildest dreams come true.

- I spend my days joyfully, at peace and fulfilled on every level.

- My loved ones are so relaxed, happy and proud of me.

- My loved ones are impressed and in awe of how my dreams always come true.

- I am like a cat. I always land on my feet

- My loved ones are in awe at my extraordinary success and happiness, and so happy for me and relaxed.

- As I win, everybody wins.

- It feels so good to generously treat my loved ones.

- I live my dream life now.

- Life is so beautiful.

- Life is so amazing.

- Life is so wondrous

- I am so lucky and blessed.

- I am living the life of my dreams and I am wildly, deeply happy.

- I have it all.

- It's normal to have it all. I am meant to have it all. There is no other shoe to drop. I am always safe, for eternity.

- It's safe for me to have it all. I am meant to have an amazing life.

- Life is meant to be fun and easy.

- Life is meant to be joyous and in the flow.

- Everyone is meant to have an amazing life.

- Everybody is meant to do what they love.

- Everybody is meant to be free.

- The more I succeed and prosper, the more it lights the way for others to do the same.

- My happiness and joy lights up the world.

- My joy and fulfillment creates a better planet.

- My success is beneficial for *everyone*. My success greatly uplifts the world.

- I add such immense, unique irreplaceable value to the Universe.

- I am generous, loving, abundant and happy.

- I love to help others where I feel called. I am so rich, successful and happy.

Positive Affirmations

- I am generous and loving. I have avalanches upon avalanches of wealth and happiness. My happiness is like a river. It never runs dry

- When I help others, my generosity and love always comes back to me a tenfold.

- I am in a sea of infinite love and prosperity

- I endlessly give and receive joy, prosperity and love

- The love I emanate comes back to me a 100x over.

- My life is filled with abundance, peace, joy and happiness.

- My life is full of freedom and expansion.

- I am FREE and fulfilled.

- I feel so good being free!!

- I do what I want to do, when I want to do it!

- I live where I want to live, and with who I want to be with.

- I travel wherever I want to go, whenever I want to go!!

- I travel the world in style, luxury and bliss.

- I am living at the peak of existence.

- I am overflowing with extraordinary freedom and divine bliss.

- I am so peaceful, blissful and fulfilled.

- I am fulfilled in ALL areas of my life.

- ALL areas of my life overflow with abundance, success and happiness.

- It feels so good to be successful and divinely fulfilled.

- I am so worthy of all my blissful success and extraordinary abundance.

- Extraordinary success and divine bliss are my birthright.

- Abundance and joy are my birthright.

- I am so worthy and deserving of this beautiful life of my dreams.

- My beautiful, blissful abundant dream life is forever.

- My beautiful, blissful life of my dreams only ever gets better and better.

- I always only ever get better and better.

- My out-of-this-world success and extraordinary abundant bliss just keep increasing and reaching new heights.

- I am always expanding and reaching the next level. There truly are no limits on my fulfillment and Oneness with the Universe. Paradise has no limits

- I am destined for permanent abundance, success, love and prosperity never-ending, forever.

Positive Affirmations

- I love life.

- Thank you God/Source/Universe for my amazing, incredible life.

- Thank you God/Source/Universe for my unbelievable success and happiness.

- Thank you so much Universe/Life/God for everything.

- I am so deeply, unbelievably blessed.

- I am always in such deep gratitude and awe.

- I have it all and it is so blissful.

- My fulfillment and success are always overflowing and multiplying. I live in permanent Heaven on Earth.

- My life will always be top, extraordinary, peak, exceptional.

- I am abundantly, ridiculously blessed now and forever.

- My life is always incredibly overflowing with divinity and success.

- I am permanently incredibly joyous and fulfilled.

- I am so thankful for my divine exceptional success, bliss and forever abundance.

- I am forever fulfilled.

- Life loves and adores me. Life protects me and always supports me.

- I am permanently divinely guided and protected.

- I trust life.

- I trust myself.

- I feel so safe and relaxed in the Universe.

- I know Life loves me.

- The Universe only ever brings me the top, very best, peak experiences in life!

- I am one with Life

- I am one with the Universe.

5.

-TALENT & CREATIVITY-

AFFIRMATIONS FOR TALENT

*T*here is an ancient Indian concept called dharma, which is linked to Divine Purpose, Destiny and one's calling!! It encompasses that each one of us is here for our own unique purpose on this Earth, and our longings and yearnings for what we wish to do directly come from our Divine dharma. Dharma is linked to the vibration of your heart!! The heart is the highest embodiment of Love, Truth, Joy and Pure Source Energy. There is only Truth and intuition to be found in the heart.

You may not think that you are here for anything special, but the fact that you are here means you are!! All dharmas are equal in value and importance. If your happiness in life is to be a stay-at-home parent, this is just as divine as a tech guru who wants to be next Elon Musk. There are no mistakes in Creation. Your dharma, longings and creative urges are leading you to your divinely designated calling and your calling is how Divinity wants to express itself through you in this lifetime. If somebody was created to want a certain thing, then that is perfect for them, for the Universe and for everybody else. When a desire comes from your heart and is your dharma, it not only serves you but also the

Highest Good of everybody! The fulfillment of your joy and your Soul's desires literally contribute to and uplift the planet! The positive high vibrations of love and fulfillment have a domino knock-on effect on the world around you. Not only are your positive feelings of satisfaction and fulfillment going out and generating more positive energy in the world; they are also directly fulfilling the needs of others. You may not know how or even be able to see how it's possible, but the Universe knows exactly how your Good will serve others for the Highest Good of all involved. Everything is connected. When you are truly living out the embodiment of your heart's desires, you will see the evidence in your own life that when you are truly happy and fulfilled, creatively expressing yourself and realizing your dreams, it directly uplifts and greatly benefits everybody else involved somehow. It truly is like Magic!

Talent and creativity can also be self-created beliefs, just like anything else. If you grew up believing you are not talented, or continuously tell yourself it is too late to do what you want to do or that you are not a natural, you are literally inadvertently creating circumstances that will mirror those false negative beliefs back to you. The Universe doesn't judge what you want. If you are saying repeatedly to yourself that you are no good at this or that or it's useless, it assumes that is what you want and then manifests it. I learnt this from Louise Hay and her excellent book "I Can Do It." However, if you change your beliefs to vibrate that you are inherently, innately talented and worthy of doing what you love, that it has been divinely assigned to you by your Creator Self and that you are endlessly supported by Life in fulfilling your unique purpose, then the evidence of that will manifest! You are in charge of what comes mirrored back to you.

One of the best books I have ever read on creativity is "The Talent Code" by Daniel Coyle. He debunks the myth that talent is determined from birth/childhood and that creative geniuses are always born prodigies. There are plenty of examples here of famous celebrated inventors and creative geniuses, sports-stars etc. who everyone assumed were naturally talented- Coyle exposes this myth by revealing the many creative failures and poor pieces of work these people produced along their journeys to mastery, showing the diligence, skill and care they really put into their craft. Talents and abilities take nurturing to develop and flourish into their highest potential.

Refuse aswell to buy into the myth of competition. What is meant for you has been divinely assigned specifically for you, and will not miss you. If something or someone you want is taken by someone else, then it wasn't the one that was meant for you- the one that is meant for you is still ahead, and it is bigger and better than what you thought you had missed!! Because life is loving and benevolent and always working towards your highest potential and happiness, what is actually meant for you is always better and far surpasses expectations for what you had originally. In the reality of Love, there is no competition- only creation. The idea of competition is an illusion that arises from false paradigms of scarcity, separation and survival!! In the vibrations of Love and the high-vibrational reality that it creates, competition doesn't exist- only abundance, creation and a limitless Universe. The Universe is so vast and limitless and can create things out of thin air that didn't even previously exist- it is so infinite and abundant that it has room for everyone's desires. The Higher Intelligence also brings people, circumstances, places and events together that are already in existence, in a harmonious way for the good of everyone involved; even if more than one person appears to want the same thing. It is never a specific thing (or person) that anyone really wants anyway- it is the essence or feeling of that desire, and the Universe has a billion and one different ways it can fulfill your desire, in ways that are far better than you even imagined! What is yours will always make a way for you. What you want, wants you even more than you want it. Everybody's unique purpose and passion on this Earth comes pre-equipped with the perfect resources, places, people and events specific and unique to them to make their dream realize. You will never need to compete for what is yours by divine right, as the Universe already has it sorted. The reason why what you want wants you even more is because the Universe specifically designed and planted your dreams and desires in your heart for a reason, and only you can fulfill them. No-one else can do what you can because it is your divine, right unique place and dharma.

If anyone tries to tell you a dream or desire is too late to start, impossible or realistic, please ignore them. They are just reflecting their own limitations and insecurities onto you! Somebody who has succeeded at fulfilling their own dreams will never tell others their dreams are unrealistic- even a dream deemed ludicrous by society such as becoming a famous singer, actor or sports-star. They will never tell you this because people who achieve outrageous dreams know that you have to be outrageous-minded to reach the stars. Impossible is nothing. With God, all things are possible. If you want to do something but fear it is too late or implausible, know that the fact that you want it at all, at any age in your life, means it is part of your Divine dharma and therefore it is meant for you. It is literally your destiny- the Divine Plan for you. The Universe will be with you every step of the way because your dharma is endlessly supported. The infamous Joseph Campbell quote "the Universe will open doors where there were only walls"- this is the power of the Life-Force moving through you, yearning to create through you.

Divine timing is also a factor in the unfolding of our destiny. You may have had a longing all your life, or spontaneously come across something new or that you'd never considered before and feel you've missed the boat. If you were meant to do what you want to do earlier, you would have done it. There are no mistakes in the Universe. There is an all-loving, all-knowing master-weaver of the fabric of your destiny over-seeing your life. Your Soul will never steer you wrong. It is only in hindsight that you will look back and see how everything works together and comes together seamlessly, in perfect divine order.

You will always find examples of people breaking limits and shattering new records! Refuse to be limited and know that Destiny is on your side. What you love and want to do is your destiny, so follow it! You are never alone. You are endlessly and lovingly supported by a Divine Higher Power that is limitless and sees everywhere- through to all the corners of this Universe and in-between, plus beyond. This Power knows exactly how to effortlessly bring the right people together, under the perfect right circumstances at the perfect right place and time.

-AFFIRMATIONS FOR CREATIVITY & TALENT-

- I am innately, uniquely talented, worthy and creative

- I am a genius at what I love to do.

- I follow my divine calling. I honor the longings within me

- I am spellbindingly talented and awed and delighted at my own abilities! I love to create

- I allow the Divinity within me to express its creativity

- I am guided by my dharma.

- I am guided by Destiny.

- I have a unique, starry destiny.

- Love, Luck and Life are on my side. Magic is on my side. I am one with the Universe

- My desire to create is really the Universe's desire for me. There is a divine plan for me. I relax and open to the guidance of Life

- I am intuitive, guided and flowing

- I respect and honor my intuition. My intuition is my best friend

- There is no-one like me. I am here for a unique purpose.

Positive Affirmations

- I create with satisfaction, deep fulfillment and love! Everything I create brings me such happiness and joy

- I feel the Creative unique energy of the Universe course through me. There is magic creative essence in my veins. I allow it to pour forth

- I am a unique, divine, holy expression of Life. I am a unique facet of the Universe's beautiful creative energy

- Nobody can do things like me. What I love is meant for me

- What I want, wants me even more

- I draw to me the perfect people at the perfect time and place who deeply value my unique talents and gifts

- I draw to me the respect and appreciation I deserve

- My gifts deserve an audience- the Universe deserves an audience.

- I allow my talents to pour forth, radiate out and touch, uplift and inspire everyone I meet!

- My talents and skills change the lives of others. I transform lives with my gifts

- My dharma serves the Highest Good of all. My unique purpose on this Earth is linked to my heart. I follow my heart

- All creativity comes from my heart. I create from my heart and Soul, knowing that everybody will be fulfilled.

- I am deeply fulfilled expressing my Art

- I feel one with the Universe

- I feel Bliss and Peace all around me. I am cocooned in the blissful, loving Flow of Life!

- The Universe constantly gives me lucky break after lucky break, surreal opportunity after surreal opportunity, to shortcut me to my destiny. Everything is easy and effortless

- I am carried in the blissful Flow of Destiny.

- I am deeply, deeply fulfilled.

6.

-LUCK & FORTUNE-

AFFIRMATIONS FOR GOOD LUCK

*L*uck is an energy, both good luck and bad luck! It is true that we are all dealt a different hand, and it is what you do with it that counts. You cannot change the hand you are dealt with, but you can always control and decide what you do with your circumstances. The power to create and shape your own life through your thoughts, decisions, actions and the creative Power you have been given as your spiritual inheritance, is far more meaningful and joyful than any hand you were dealt with at birth in the physical world.

You cannot be a victim and a winner at the same time. You cannot be loved by the Universe and a victim at the same time. You have to make a choice, and so if you want to be a Winner and have good luck and be loved by Life, then choose now to let go of victimhood. It is no big loss~ what we gain in return is far greater, more empowering, and fun!

-LUCK & GRATITUDE-

It is also worth noting that the <u>vibration of Gratitude</u> is a strong signal that vibrates good luck and fortune. When you practise energy of Gratitude, it sends out the signal of: "I have received good things. Life loves me [it must do, in order to give me this/do this for me]." When you genuinely feel gratitude, for example when you are doing a gratitude list and really feeling it, it is telling the Universe that you feel grateful because Life has blessed you with something- there is something good in your life that has been given to you. Life didn't *have to* give you this thing, place, person or experience, but it *did*, and you feel grateful. Sincerely striving to cultivate the energy of gratitude in your life will establish and strengthen a consistent vibration of daily miracles in your life. You are sending out a lucky energy of Life loving you and giving you good things, which in turn will invite more of it. When we acknowledge that Life is giving us generous gifts, big and small, and we feel truly thankful and joyous, we send that energy signature of gratitude out into the Universe! The Universe responds in kind by bringing us back more things, people, places, circumstances and events to feel joyful and happy about, because it is matching our vibration. Give out good and more good will come back to you.

-LUCK & OPPORTUNITIES-

The best book I have ever read about creating good luck is "*The Luck Factor*" by Richard Wiseman. If you want to know more about how to increase your luck, especially from a psychological point of view, I would recommend this book as first port of call.

A very interesting point made by this book is that opportunities come through people. Therefore, if you want to increase your luck, connect with people as much as you can because the Universe has a clear and easy channel to deliver the fulfillment of what you asked for via people. Because the Universe is non-corporeal, it uses people to deliver its messages or blessings or the fulfillment of your desires. For example, your dream job will come through an employer from the Universe. If you meet your soulmate, well obviously they are a tangible physical person, and it might be that you meet through mutual friends or at a party- other people have to invite you to the party or organize the get-together. Saying this, the Universe can and does work miracles so if you really can't get yourself out there for whatever reason then it will still bring the right people and events to you to fulfill your desire. It's more just about doing your best. We all know where our limit is. As long as we do our best; our part of the inspired action, then we have done enough. By doing your part to the best of your ability, you are showing openness, willingness and courage to the Universe and it is this willingness and courage to pursue your dreams that is rewarded.

-AFFIRMATIONS FOR GOOD LUCK-

- I am so lucky.

- I am the luckiest person I know!

- Good fortune follows me wherever I go

- Life loves me

- I am so loved by Life!

- I am a favorite of Life

- I am deeply loved by the Universe

- I have the magic touch

- Everything I touch turns to magic, vibrant Energy

- I leave magic in my wake wherever I go

- I am embued with lucky, dazzling fortune energy

- My good fortune is great

- I am the luckiest person ever to have lived

- I am the luckiest person ever!

- I have a grand Destiny

- I have a starry Destiny

- I am divinely protected and blessed always

Positive Affirmations

- Wherever I go, I am divinely protected, safe and supported on my journey

- I am on a hero's journey

- I am a hero

- I love myself

- I am a Winner

- I always win at life

- Things always just get better and better for me

- I always go from strength to strength, winning to winning

- My life is tumultuous with blessings

- My life is rained upon with heavenly, gorgeous delightful blessings

- My life is a lucky charm

- I radiate beauty, health, charm, exquisiteness, radiant joy and love

- I am my own best friend

- I can do anything

- I am outrageously blessed

- I love and believe in myself, always.

- LUCK & FORTUNE-

- Luck is on my side

- I win anything I turn my hand to

- I was blessed by the Gods

- I am divinely protected, magical and with divine purpose

- Life protects, supports and guides me on my journey

- Why am I so lucky?

- Why am I so blessed?

- It feels so good to be so lucky all the time!

- I know I am always safe

- I am outrageously blessed with good fortune

- Life carries me effortlessly through the outrageous slings and arrows of fortune

- I sail through life on the winds of outrageous good Luck and Fortune

- I am carried on the wings of Good Fortune

- The God-Force is with me wherever I go

- I am supernaturally lucky

- My luck is out of this world

- I am in awe, gratitude and delight for my good luck!

Positive Affirmations

- I am lucky wherever I go

- I am always divinely safe and protected

- I am so truly lucky in life

- I am pure luck

- I radiate Magic energy

- There is no other shoe to drop

- Life just gets better and better. I am eternally out of this world lucky

- I live a magic life

- I know it's just me and the Universe. I am the only Power in my world, and I am Safe.

- LUCK & FORTUNE-

7.

-FRIENDSHIPS AND FORGIVENESS-

*T*his is a quick chapter on friendships, relationships, forgiveness and moving on.

I have noticed that the closer and more harmonious you feel with the Universe/your Self/Higher Power, the better quality your relationships are; friendships, work relationships, the people you meet out in the world, what you attract etc. Simultaneously, when our connection with the Universe/Self/Higher Power is fraught or lacking, quarrels and disconnection often arise in our friendships and relationships. The Universe is non-corporeal and works through people. The easiest way for the Universe to demonstrate its love for you is via people- by sending you loving, harmonious, positive friends and loves that are good for you and who reflect the qualities of the relationship you have with the Universe. If you have a difficult relationship with the Universe, for example if you distrust the Universe or think it is spiteful, you will attract people in your life who are untrustworthy and mean. If you want to change this then work on changing how you see the Universe. If you desire supportive and fun friends, then work on the feeling that the Universe is deeply supportive of you, that it wants you to have fun and that life is meant to be fun and easy all the time! (This is actually do-able. I have seen it, and lived it! If you are open to it, you will allow it in.) When you deeply love the Universe and feel it loving you back, you know that you are always safe and that people are just reflections of the Love you have with the Universe. You are never alone because you always have your Higher Power.

Know aswell that if people leave your life, especially when you go through something very tough, then those people were ultimately not for your Highest Good! We meet people for a reason, a season or a lifetime. It is not a failure if a friendship or relationship does not last forever. It means that both people got what they needed to out of the relationship at a soul level, and now it is time to move on. The Universe will **never**, ever take people from you without plans to fill the void with better and more loving, generous, kind-hearted, fun high-vibrational people that are good for you and more in line with the direction you are going. This is true even for the most painful breakups and loss of friendships. You might not be able to see it for a while, but even those ended for your Highest Good. Your highest happiness and growth are your Soul's *raison d'être* in this life, so know that you are divinely protected and divinely guided at all times. Your Soul will not let people leave your life who are aligned with your Highest Good and new (better) future, and if they really are aligned with your Truth and they still leave, then they will come back later anyway.

Do not be afraid to lose people. It is true that we have soul friends, soulmates, soul family etc. who carry a more permanent bond in our lives. Usually we meet these special people through heart bonds; when we are in Love vibration it attracts our soul family, soul friends, soul lovers etc. and because the vibration is so profound and heart-felt, heart bonds formed from love vibrations tend to be permanent, long-lasting, durable, forgiving and graceful- meaning your soul friends will still be there for you through the worst times. If there is an instance where you fall out, you will eventually make up but there will be zero resentment on both sides; it'll be as if the falling out never happened! It isn't like a normal relationship where you forgive but don't forget. With soulmate friendships, relationships or any other type of heart and soul bond, when the forgiveness occurs, it's as if the incident never happened and the forgetting portion will naturally take care of itself! Relationships born from soul and heart bonds are very innocent, pure and in the present moment. That is the essence of pure Love and understanding, and it is present in heart and soul friends and relationships. It is as if the past doesn't exist and the moment is just pure, present and new.

However, sometimes there are instances where we have soul friends who are bonded through the heart and they still move on or the friendship 'goes wrong,' or they are nowhere to be found when you need them! This doesn't mean you have done anything wrong! It just means that you are moving to a higher place, the next stage of your evolution, and those people couldn't go with you to where you are going next. Maybe they are at different stages of their lives or have different lessons. It does not mean the friendship or the relationship was any less real. It just means that there are even better friends waiting ahead for you, and they will be even more loving and aligned with your heart and soul's purpose than the old ones! It can be hard to believe when you've shared a really deep bond with someone and have so many happy, loving experiences together, but it really is true! Life is always moving towards a better and higher fulfillment and expression of itself, and the heart is always opening deeper and deeper to Love, because that is the heart's reason for existing in this lifetime. Not only does life move towards more expansion and fulfillment; the heart also moves towards a richer depth and deeper fathoms of Love. Your new soul friends will be even more exciting, even more loving, even more genuine, fulfilling and fun, supportive, generous, kind, understanding and any other quality you value in a true friend.

Never be afraid to lose anyone or anything, because in the reality of Spirit everything is formless. It may get concentrated and solidified into a form, i.e. "manifested," when it is materialized on this plane in the forms of people as well as everything else. We all have our soul friends, soulmates, and dream manifestations and yet they are still just representations of a vibration we have sent out. Nobody has the ultimate power over you to be your Source. The Universe and your own Higher Self are your Source. You are the Source of Love in your world. You are the one who carries Love inside you, has the power to connect to Divine Love and to radiate love out into the Universe, which comes back to you in like form. The best anyone ever is is just a form of an energy you have sent out- they may be a very good form, but at the end of the day they are still just a form. You are the Power and the Love of the Universe, and you have the Power to be and give out love and receive love back to you as much as you want. There are no limits to love- it truly is a boundless, infinite creative energy; with limitless forms and possibilities.

There may be a period of nothingness in-between where the old people have left your life and the new ones haven't arrived yet. This is okay. The void is a place of great mystery, possibility and potential. It is silent and quiet and seemingly empty, yet in reality it is actually teeming with the new seeds of Creation. The darkness is peaceful, silent and all-knowing. At the heart of the darkness lies infinity and creation. The light is born from the same place as the dark; they are One- Yin-and-Yang. It is a place of pure potentiality, incredible limitless possibilities, infinite expansion and creation. What it promises is always so much bigger and better than what was left behind. It is Nature's promise to you as an extension of itself that the best in life is always yet to come.

-FORGIVENESS & LOVE-

There are lots of different methods to forgive someone or something. You can try the Hawaiian Ho'oponopono prayer "I forgive you, I'm sorry, Thank you, I love you." In my experience, this prayer has worked via cognitive behavioral therapy- when I thought about the person or situation I wanted to forgive and repeated each phrase, my mind instantly came up with a justification for the healing mantra I was saying. For example, "Tom, I forgive you/I am choosing to forgive you, *because it's not your fault you weren't who I thought you would be. Tom, I am sorry that we had to go through this lesson together, because I know it was probably painful for you too. Tom, thank you for showing me how strong I was and giving me a chance to keep my word to myself.* Tom, I love you *because you were a major part of my spiritual growth and you made me more into the person I'm meant to become.*" The base mantra "I forgive you, I'm sorry, Thank you, I love you" remains the same, but the mind comes up with a positive unique healing thought to follow each segment of the mantra specific to the individual's situation. I thoroughly believe that all bad feelings can be traced back to specific thoughts, and when you change the thought, the feeling follows. When you change the feeling, the energy in you, around you and around that other person also changes. We are all interconnected.

You can also try positive affirmations for forgiveness! The best forgiveness affirmation I have heard is something like: "I am *willing* to forgive. I do not know *how*, but the Universe will handle it for me". This is something I picked up from Louise Hay's "*Trust Life*" set of affirmations that was released after her death! It works especially best when you want to or are willing to forgive someone, but you can't bring yourself to do it or don't know how to. Sometimes a resentment is so strong that we feel begrudging to forgive someone- acknowledging that we don't know how to forgive sets us free from pressuring ourselves to be able to do something so demanding. Often we have been treated unfairly by someone and that's why we are having to forgive in the first place!!

Ultimately the purpose of forgiving someone who has done you wrong is to free *yourself* from the dense, heavy energy of resentment!! The heart chakra carries the hurt and this clogs up its precious space, blocking more love from coming in. Kimberly Snyder says in her book "*You Are More Than You Think You Are*" that resentments are literally energy knots in the auric field and forgiving someone is akin to releasing a big muscle knot!! This is such a good analogy. When you do genuinely manage to release that energetic burden and truly feel forgiveness towards someone, often you physically feel a lightening and expansion of your energy field!! These sensations and feelings are openings and liftings of your energy space!! When you release those lower, hurtful vibrations, you are raising your energy field to a higher frequency and becoming a match instead to the frequencies of love, good and joy!!

Another excellent way to experience forgiveness and to lighten your own energy field is to write a gratitude list of everything good that the experience with this person or situation has taught you!! Gratitude, along with Love, is the king of all feel-good energies. Often, hurts and heartbreaks turn out to be life lessons that ultimately shape us into the person we are meant to be- our truest, most powerful, loving and wisest selves!! Ultimately, our destiny is always moving into greater and more love. Every grievance and hurt you experience ultimately opens you up to more and more love. These experiences are not here to harden your heart and make you "stronger"- not in the way that is commonly thought of anyway. A lot of the time, whilst they are still opportunities to learn to strengthen and assert your boundaries and strengthen your self-esteem- at the same time they aren't designed to keep people out or to keep love and friendship away from you! On the contrary, whilst they are designed to strengthen your self-confidence and self-worth in the way that you realize how you are worthy of being treated- at the same time they are here to make you even more loving, even more compassionate, even more open and connected to others and even more open and magnetic to love!!

If you are having a hard time letting go or forgiving, when all else fails, focus on Love! Relax into the energy of the Love of the Universe. The Love vibration tends to make you softer, more forgiving and open and receptive to the love of the Universe. The love of the Universe comes through and shows up via people! Receiving, being open to and allowing more Love to move through you will often cause you to see a different and more understanding perception regarding the person you want to forgive- and it may also make you realize that you deserve better and to cut that person from your life going forward!! Forgiveness doesn't always mean letting someone back into your life. Loving yourself goes hand-in-hand with the most loving, positive transcendent energies of Life, and so sometimes when we are truly immersed in Love energy, the intuition we get may be to cut ties with that person!! This is still loving- it is just more loving to yourself. The person who you release will also be fine in the long-run- in fact, they will be better for it! What is for your Highest Good is also for the Higher Good of everyone else. When we are released by somebody, whilst it temporarily feels like a loss, in the long-run we always end up somehow benefitting! When someone releases us, they are setting us free to move onto and receive our Higher Good and the next best people who are right for us! If someone is truly meant to be in your life; whether it is a lover, a friend or some other type of relationship, then they will come back around even after you release them. In these cases, where it is meant to be, forgiveness will be natural and easy and genuine- meaning that when you think about the incident ever again in future, neither side will genuinely not hold any resentment anymore- it'll be almost like it never happened. This is forgiveness and true Love in action, and often happens between soul families, soulmates and soul friends (and soul colleagues, soul clients etc.). It is spontaneous normally, and you won't even have to try!

However, if you are immersed in a loving energy and that person still says or does something that irritates you, then most likely that person is not meant to be for your Highest Good, and it's best to gently release them and move forward with the people- and new people coming- who are meant to be in your new life!! Some of our connections- even if they are soul friends for a short time or medium-term, are meant to be transitory, for a season, or to teach or give you something, develop you in some way, be there for you etc. and then go. The soul contract is completed. It is not a failure on either side; it's just that you experienced what you were meant to with that person and now it's time to move on to the next stage of your destiny!!

8.

- MIRACLES, WISHES FULFILLED & DREAMS COMING TRUE -

AFFIRMATIONS FOR MIRACLES

his is a brief segment of affirmations for when you go through a challenging period in life and would like things to turn around for you!! These affirmations are for miracles and good things happening out of the blue.

Remember that these dark periods do not last, even if often they seem to last much longer than we would like! Everything happens for a reason and in the end even the darker times will serve you. We experience our most tremendous growth through the toughest challenges. Like a beautiful lotus flower growing from the mud, the sweet chestnut seeds germinating underneath the cold, dark winter soil or the beautiful transcendent butterflies emerging strong with their stunning wings from their cocoons. All of these creatures in Nature require their unique, individual struggle to grow and become who they're meant to be!

I am not trying to say that life necessarily has to be hard or that struggle is absolutely mandatory to grow. At the same time though, I think if a challenge has already occurred or is happening, then we may as well recognize and utilize it as another opportunity for growth! I actually believe that part of the journey is ultimately realizing that struggle and suffering are no longer always necessary for our growth and fulfillment. However, we won't come to deeply understand this until we've gone through the experience several times. It can take several dark nights of the Soul and subsequent spiritual awakenings to become fully aware of and awaken to our own true Power; the Power within us, God. With God, all things are possible.

When we stand forth in the Radiance of our own Power, we are stronger and better equipped to move through challenges and know they are happening for a reason. We are the Light that illuminates the dark. No matter what, we always have our inner strength and our Higher Power to guide us, even if it looks like it isn't there in the darkness. It is only in retrospect when we look back that we can see God was there in it with us all along. There is an anonymous poem: *"Footprints in the Sand,"* that demonstrates this perfectly.

I think too that there is an element of "what you give out, you get back". Therefore, if we are going around focused on and invested in the idea of challenges and pain being necessary for our growth or just because we think it's how it has to be, then we will create a life where obstacles are never-ending, challenges and struggle are always in sight etc.

Perhaps there may always seem to be challenges, because as humans we don't stay positive 100% of the time. However, by fully accepting and embracing and allowing our most difficult feelings during the darker periods, ironically we are actually being more positive because we allow and honor space for our feelings!

Honoring your negative feelings and allowing yourself to be vulnerable allows room for Grace and miracles and acknowledges the fact that we are not alone in our grief. Life is there for us, to hold us even during the worst times.

When we are in a barren desert state, often there isn't much inspiration, so we just have to do the best we can and take any idea that feels vaguely good to us, even if it's just "okay." This is fine. Don't be afraid to move forward just because the action steps you can muster aren't "inspired" or perfect. I made this mistake for a very long time. I was so used to being high-vibrational and having obvious/magical inspired action as a result of that, that when I found myself in this desert space again, I was indignant at having to take so-called uninspired actions as I saw it as totally pointless without the high vibrations behind it! I did not move forward for two years. Eventually, I was lucky enough that my therapist Claire Winchester, who is one of the best things that ever happened to me, said "we are meant to make mistakes, it's part of the learning process, that's how you move forward and grow." I realized she was right. Looking back, even though I did hardly anything for two years, the tiny action steps I did force myself to take out of sheer boredom and frustration (even though I knew they weren't inspired) did not work out like a high-vibrational inspired action does; however they still moved me forward in the direction of my goals as they taught me something valuable and moved me in a direction. Taking messy imperfect action to the best of your current ability is better than standing completely still and waiting. Taking messy action, taking risks and making mistakes is an admirable and courageous thing to do. The Universe appreciates the effort and it is better than sitting around waiting for Grace to show up again, because we don't know when exactly the Universe will decide to make its presence known again. We can also elevate our state the best we can to try and encourage inspiration to show up, as inspired action often comes through high vibration. There are times though, where despite our best efforts, it is so challenging to feel good due to external overwhelming life circumstances. The Universe knows this, and will always meet us halfway as we do the best we can. If we know we are doing our best, even if it isn't to the degree to which we can normally create when we are happy, then that is more than enough. Inspiration and Grace show up aswell when we are in a complete and utter state of Surrender; when we cannot help ourselves this is when the Universe does and will help you. No matter what, things will work out. Believe in yourself and believe in the Universe!

When we can muster strength, we can begin to take baby steps forward in any direction that feels good to us. It's okay if we can only see the first 5-10 feet ahead of us in the dark. We don't have to see the whole road to move forward; this is where your Faith kicks in. Know that there is a Higher Power that loves you and knows exactly where you need to go! It may take a few mis-steps and directions- just keep moving. Know that every step forward is leading you to somewhere, and as long as you keep going, everything will add up and be useful in where you're going in ways you can't even see yet, and you will reach your Destination. Nothing is wasted in the Universe.

Do not be scared if it seems like two steps forward, ten steps back. This is a period of new beginnings, grieving and endings, mixing and integrating the two to bring forth new life. You can feel bursts of excitement, new possibilities, happiness and hope and optimism and have it dispersed with periods of great grief, sadness, despair etc. There is room for all of your emotions. Allow and honor all of them. This is a journey as old as time that every human goes through; it is even in the Old Testament- *Exodus* and I am sure there are other variations in other ancient religious texts. One day, it does end and you do reach your Promised Land.

Believe in yourself and the inevitable Grace and support of the Universe. There is a Higher Power who is conspiring for all events to work out beautifully in your favor and in the most magical ways in the end.

-AFFIRMATIONS FOR MIRACLES-

- My life is getting better and better

- Miracle after miracle is popping into my life

- Blessings upon blessings are raining down on me, slowly then faster and faster!

- It feels so good to receive

- I am divinely taken care of and blessed. I see things magically turning around for me

- Life is Good. The Universe is good. I am loved and cared for and safe

- I am always perfectly protected in the Universe

- Everything works out for me

- I am taken to where I need to be

- Life is always guiding me, step by step, even in the darkness.

- I love life. I am happy to be alive!

- I can always trust the Universe

- Life has a plan for me. Everything serves my ultimate good and takes me to my destiny

- I am always where I need to be, at the perfect place and at the perfect time.

Positive Affirmations

- Everything serves my Higher Purpose

- My Growth and potential are maximized. I use this experience for my highest growth and greatest good

- I trust life. I am always carried to where I need to be in perfect divine timing.

- There is nothing but Love and Good in the Universe. Everything serves me. Everything happens *for* me.

- I am divinely blessed, perfectly protected and guided.

- There is a notable upswing in my Fortune. My life is permanently taking a turn for the better

- Life loves me. I now receive miracle after miracle, divine blessing after divine blessing

- Good things are starting to happen now for me, even better than I could have ever imagined!

- Miracle after miracle now comes rushing into my reality, in quick succession!

- Miracles and divine extravagant blessings just pop and pour into my reality!

- Things work out for me in the most jaw-dropping ways, even better beyond my wildest dreams!

- I am surprised and delighted by all the good that is pouring and pouring into my life!

- Life is SO loving and generous with me.

- Life now just goes from strength to strength, wild success to wild success- always better and better.

- Only and all good ever comes to me now.

- I relax as I now move into my Greater Good.

- I feel so relaxed, safe, loved and cared for and secure in the Universe.

- Everything always works out for me. I am cocooned in love and bliss.

- I am so supported by the Universe. I am feeling *one* with Life

- I trust Life. I am grateful for all the good that continues to rush in!

- Larger and larger, more extravagant sums of money come pouring in. There is always overflow

- Huge sums of income continue to show up to bless and prosper me. Money is my friend. I am so supported and cared for by Life.

- I allow extravagant, outrageous abundance into my life

- My life only ever gets better and better.

- The love in my life only ever grows greater and greater

- More and more love fills my life

Positive Affirmations

- I am overflowing with love. The Universe loves me

- I am so relaxed, happy, peaceful, safe and secure wherever I am in life.

- I live in complete freedom, luxury, love, abundance, bliss and Oneness where I am

- Everything is well.

9.

-BEAUTY AND SELF-CONFIDENCE-

AFFIRMATIONS FOR BEAUTY

*T*his chapter is about beauty and self-confidence-feeling good about yourself and loving and appreciating the unique gift of who you are!! When we feel beautiful and confident on the inside, we radiate beauty and magnetism on the outside and we attract all people, places, circumstances and things that are a match to our highest positive feelings about ourselves. Feeling beautiful and empowered in who you are is a decision you make. As you are the only one who creates in your reality, the only one who decides you are beautiful is **you.**

-DREAM BODY-

If you desire any physical changes in your appearance or a certain look, then feeling good about yourself first is the quickest way to get there. By feeling good about yourself and loving who you are, any changes that need to be made in external physical reality to match that will take care of themselves! The Universe shifts and rearranges reality to match the vibration you are putting out. When you practice a regular vibration of loving who you are and how you look, the Universe creates a reality that mirrors your own self-confidence and love for yourself!

The Truth of your body reflects the inner You. When you make changes from a place of alignment with your True Self, your body will be of divine inspiration and not from ego. When you connect with your Higher Self, the vision of you will come from the Truth of your heart and any changes that arise from that will lead to a truer reflection of the Inner You.

If you didn't know what you wanted and simply allowed Source Energy to move through you, the highest expression of yourself would manifest anyway, because the Intelligence of Divine Wisdom knows what will make us happy and truly fulfill us even better than we do! As you fully connect with Source, the Universe naturally radiates the highest, truest and most beautiful authentic expression of you. Changes that unfold from a place of being connected to your Higher Self and to Source will always result in the most beautiful and magnetic version of you. Any physical and practical actions you are inspired to take will be fun, easy and effortless!

If you do have a clear and authentic heart-based goal for what you want, then you can set out to achieve this using traditional goal-setting. This includes visualization, scripting and/or affirmations! We all have different ways of positively entraining our minds to focus on our goals. The best method is the one that helps you to keep your mind focused to the extent that you can vividly feel how it would be when you attain your goal! Vividly imagine how it would look and feel if you were already exactly how you always wanted to be and your own ideal. Practise feeling the vibrations of love, deep gratitude, joy and delight for your body! You will begin to attract people, situations, circumstances and events that mirror your own positive self-loving thoughts back to you. Feeling grateful, overjoyed and delighted for your unique beauty inside and out radiates out an energy into the Universe that says: "I am extremely gorgeous inside and out, and I love the way I look and feel!"

Michael James, author of *"Feel Better, No Matter What!"* says: "feel beautiful first, and the mirror of external reality, including your body and other people, will reflect it back to you."

You don't need to worry or concern yourself about how your dream body will manifest. The Universe will take care of *how* your new positive, self-loving thoughts and feelings materialize! The way in which the outside world changes to meet your desires will be deeply fulfilling, as you are sending out the feelings of deep fulfillment and joy to the Universe and so the physical reality that manifests has to match the quality of those feelings.

Something else I learnt from Michael James is that how other people see you also comes from within. He has an exercise where you list all the times you felt beautiful/attractive, including the times you received compliments from others. When I did this exercise, I found that 9 times out of 10 whenever I received a compliment, it traced back to me feeling good *first*- either very happy or high-vibrational in general, or feeling good about myself! The times that you attract the most and best people into your life who admire and appreciate your unique qualities are the times where you have been radiating out feelings of self-appreciation and celebration first! Other people then pick up on that positive wavelength and enter your life, reinforcing your own positive feelings about yourself with their words and treatment of you!

As you feel very close to the Universe and connected to Source, you radiate your True Self and this is when you are at your most beautiful, attractive and magnetic. When you stand in and radiate your Truth, you energetically draw people in who are a match to your highest and happiest Self! You are truly radiant and at your most gorgeous and desirable when you are closely connected to Source! Feeling close to or even one with your Higher Self makes you beautiful, magnetic and enchanting. Source Energy is so irresistible and entrancing to everyone and it is within **_all_** of us. We all have access to this most powerful, magnetic, beautiful and transcendent energy in the Universe. All you need to do is connect to Source; your Higher Self.

Being one with Source also magnetizes the right soul people who you love and adore into your life, who also love and adore you! Because Source Energy is pure love, joy and fulfillment, as you radiate the joy of Source you will also attract the perfect soul people to you who mirror those feelings of love, Oneness, fulfillment and joy back to you!! Afterall, you can only really feel deep and true fulfillment when you are with your perfect right soul people and situations for you. Not only does this mean attracting people who love and admire you for your unique self; it also means attracting the perfect people you love, appreciate and admire _back_. Soul love in all forms- friends, colleagues, lovers, associates etc. is very mutual. When you find fulfillment and Love within you by first connecting to your True Self and the Love of Source, you will magnetize your soul people and the right places, situations, circumstances and events that match your Oneness and deep fulfillment within will unfold.

You are the Source of Love and Paradise, and Love and Paradise are within you all the time.

-COMPETITION & UNIQUENESS-

My friend Ryan once told me "you have to remember aswell that everybody has different eyes." It was only till some years later that I came to understand what he meant. Everybody has a different idea of what they find attractive and beautiful. I had a friend who involuntarily made a grimace/disgusted face once when I admiringly showed him a photo of a Victoria's Secret model, who at the time was the society ideal of beauty! My boyfriend at the time had the same reaction, and both told me that they didn't find the completely flat, toned stomach of the model attractive, and they found it very sexy when a woman has little rolls of fat around the waist and stomach! This is the opposite of what society at the time was pushing as attractive. The society ideal is always changing, and as I write this book in 2022, the Victoria's Secret model slim/athletic physique has already been replaced by the new current social media trend. It has been this way for centuries, and in another 5 years, the current trend will be replaced by something else. This is why it is important to love how **you** specifically look, admire and appreciate your own unique self and feel happy and fulfilled by *you* to the point where you never want to be anyone else! *You* are your own ideal. When you are the number one 'idol' in your life, it is bliss.

We all have unique traits, both physical and internally that make us stunningly, eye-catchingly beautiful and more importantly-heart-capturingly beautiful. Beauty is not about how somebody looks purely physically but it is about how they make you *feel*. This is why inner beauty is so important and will always transcend outer appearances.

When we celebrate the unique gift of who we are, we tap into an energy of gratitude and recognition that we have been created with divine Love and careful consideration! We are all unique and divine creative expressions of Life. I believe we were designed exactly on purpose the way we are for a reason, and a lot of thought has gone into our unique physical traits, characteristics, personalities and individual talents, gifts and interests!! Beauty is an amalgamation of the body, heart, mind, spirit and soul.

Our bodies are uniquely designed vessels for our souls that reflect the inner us. I believe sometimes even our features are chosen to express and reflect our inner beauty, e.g. someone who is very playful, fun-loving and light-hearted may have radiant skin or softer, more child-like features. Someone who is more serious or mysterious may have more chiseled/fine-boned features or piercing eyes. Some people even look like the careers they lovingly chose- e.g. a primatologist who looks slightly ape-like (in a beautiful way!).

Life loves diversity and uniqueness amongst its Creation. Variety, individuality and everyone co-existing harmoniously, perfectly complementing and strengthening each other symbiotically- this is the Love and Beauty of the Universe. A mysterious, sleek black panther is just as striking and beautiful as a colorful, showy bird of paradise. A rose is just as ethereally beautiful and visually stunning as a lily (Miranda Kerr, "*Treasure Yourself*"). Even plants and animals from the same species are never exactly alike! There are always variations between individuals, for example, in humans no identical twins ever have the same fingerprints as one another. In Nature, no rock ever has the exact same texture, form or markings as another, no tree ever has the exact same twist to its branches or interplay of colors woven amongst its canopy of foliage and no snowflake will ever be exactly like the one that came before it or another one in future!! No sunset will ever quite be the same as another one before that has set the sky extraordinarily on fire. Nature never re-creates anyone or anything exactly the same, therefore each creation is very special and utterly unique.

If you have ever felt jealous of another, it's only because you're not feeling fully fulfilled within yourself and your own unique expression of that thing. For example, if you ever felt jealous of someone else's body, it's because you're not feeling that you're fully expressing your own fullest potential when it comes to your body. What you are actually wanting and admiring is the most beautiful and feel-good version of your own body! This is true in all areas of life- not just body but also your career, money, lifestyle and wealth etc. You never actually want someone else's looks, talents, creativity, job, car or house etc., but rather you want your own best version of that. So know that if you ever do feel jealous, it's only showing you what you need to work on developing for yourself. Sometimes, especially when it comes to our bodies and how we look, what we actually need to work on developing for ourselves is our confidence rather than actually acquiring physical changes. Too often, we are already gifted with the most incredible and rare beauty but we fail to see it! Everybody is beautiful and special in their own unique way. Everybody has equal value because we were all created with a purpose. God would not have created different shapes, sizes, skin tones, features, personality traits etc. if each one did not have equal beauty and merit. As humans, we have created judgments and ignored the fact that everybody has different tastes and that beauty is truly in the eye of the beholder. There is no "society norm" that is more powerful than True Beauty- the truth that everybody is equally worthy, beautiful and special in their own way. When you accept this, you will find it easier to fully love, accept and enjoy yourself and know that if anyone tries to make you feel less than beautiful, it is because they are the wrong people and you are probably in the wrong environment!

Your own unique Self is 1000x more beautiful, magnetic and interesting than if you were just a carbon copy of everybody else. As you are fully happy with yourself and realizing your own best potential, jealousy dissipates.

Coming back to the idea that that everybody has different eyes....there is somebody for everyone. Each person has an ideal that they find the most attractive for *them*! Every individual has a unique set of friends, lovers, soulmate, colleagues, clients etc. who they find the best and most ideal people for them. Objectively, "the best" cannot actually exist, because even for people who are voted the most beautiful celebrity of the year, there is always at least a few people out there who don't find them appealing at all. I have met people who didn't find some of these celebrities attractive for the very features that made them famous in the first place! We all have individual preferences, and I believe that we are all perfectly and deliberately designed exactly how we are in order to make us the most attractive to our soulmates and soul people!! The very features that some people may have rejected you for will be the exact same features that your soulmate and soul people will be crazy about and find most special about you!! This doesn't just apply to physical traits but also your personality and your spirit!! Your soulmate and soul people will prefer you above all others and think that **you** are the most beautiful/gorgeous and attractive person they've ever seen inside and out- and you will also feel the same about them!! Soul connections are *very* mutual. That is one of the reasons why they are so magical and transcendent. They are born from Love and a very high-vibrational energy and so of course they are perfect. The Universe has created love, friendships and all other relationships in such a Divine matrix of Harmony that soul people genuinely find each other their best and most perfect ideal, and would never choose anybody else! With soulmates of any nature- soul lovers, soul friends, soul clients, soul colleagues etc. the fit is always mutual and perfect and the feelings are peak, extraordinary and magical! You are the most gorgeous, beautiful and attractive person inside and out to your soul people, and they are the most attractive, gorgeous and best people to you!

-SELF-ACCEPTANCE-

There are no flaws or accidents in Nature. What are now often deemed as "flaws" in our culture are often just normal variations of features! There are a variety of different features, skin tones, hair colors, eye colors, sizes, shapes, face structures etc. and all are individual and unique. I believe true beauty comes from accepting and embracing what you have been given and accepting that it has been given to you for a reason. You are perfect in the Universe's eyes and very special, gifted and beautiful! There is a unique gift in what you have to offer and you are a divine miracle. When you accept that you are perfect exactly as you are and embrace that you were created the way you were for a reason, you will find it easier to celebrate, love and appreciate yourself! As you love yourself deeply on this level and see yourself as unique and special and wonderful, you will find it easier to attract people on your same wavelength who adore you and see the specialness of who you are!

There is nobody who is "perfect" externally. If you look at a celebrity who is commonly perceived as very beautiful or someone you find very attractive in real life, you will find that if you really analyze them close up you will find at least 2-3 things wrong with them. Flaws do not detract away from the overall beauty of a person. Beauty is an energy that animates the body and the environment around, including other people. Beauty comes from within and is decided by the person. People who are very beautiful or attractive are the ones who have simply decided they are. Empowerment comes from within.

Flaws and vulnerabilities are also what endear us to others! We love people more when they show they are not perfect and show us their vulnerabilities and insecurities. Sad times can really connect us on a human level. Human relationships echo our relationships with the Universe and so just as we are deeply loved by the Universe when we have moments of weakness and vulnerability, we are also loved and cared for on a deeper, more genuine and authentic level by people when they see we need help. As we show we are not perfect and have flaws and insecurities, people love us more, not less, and can relate to us, which brings us closer. There is nobody on this Earth who does not have flaws, imperfections, vulnerabilities and insecurities.

Love as an energetic field is so powerfully transcendent and magnetic that it rapidly outshines everything on a purely superficial level. Love is the very fabric of the Universe; a powerful Force that includes *everyone*. Love is completely free from fear, judgment, criticism and division. The luminescence of Love is so dazzlingly transcendent and high-vibrational that it quickly outshines anything biologically 'lacking' on the outside. There are animals in the wild who have missing eyes, ears, limbs, scars etc., but they are still whole, perfect and complete and they know it doesn't take away from their worth. They don't let it get them down as they know that they are still beautiful, perfect and lovable! Animals are generally at a purer state of Love than humans as they are free from judgments, over-thinking and negative conditioning/unnatural lifestyles that take them away from their primitive roots. Love is a primal Force that is synonymous with Truth. These animals still always end up with the mates they're destined to be with because they are closer to Love and Truth. Lots of natural animals have physical defects actually, because they are living out in in the wilderness of Nature where accidents, injuries and diseases etc. are always happening as a part of that.

A lot of the time, someone's flaws, e.g. scars or stomach stretchmarks from emotional eating, make them cute and endearing to the people that love them- they are a sign of vulnerability and that someone has had challenges. There is something deeply attractive about vulnerability. You may not like your scars precisely *because* they are reminders of times you'd rather forget, and I understand that. However, life fundamentally has meaning and a story- and every great story has ups, downs and contrast. The boring or unpleasant parts of a story always enhance and serve the glorious parts in the grander context of the story arc as a whole. It's like a song where the quieter beats or build-ups break through into exhilarating drops or crescendos- the impact of the drop or crescendo isn't as hard-hitting without the subdued build-up beforehand. This is like life.

Sometimes the shame we feel around life events or our mistakes can translate into feelings of shame around our bodies. When we replace shame and regret around a situation or memory with self- approval and even pride, these positive feelings heal the energy of shame around our bodies. On accepting and even approving of our past shames and most catastrophic mistakes; seeing them as learning experiences or necessary parts of our journey, we bring self-love and pride to the energy fields around our beings. These self-loving feelings of pride and approval will show up and reflect in our external health and beauty aswell.

Going back to Nature and animals as an example, animals refuse to feel shame or see themselves as 'lacking' for what they've been through. Sometimes, an animal's scars or missing limbs make them even more interesting, cooler and attractive because their bodies physically depict the story of their adventure in life; their interaction and dance with the elements of Nature, their strength after conquering their challenges and their connection with the Flow of the Story of Life. Another thing my friend Ryan said once was "I'd rather arrive at the end of my life with a banged up body and enjoyed the ride than arrive there in a perfect body and never have lived!"

-PHOTOGENICITY-

Photogenicity in my opinion is directly correlated to happiness and confidence! When you are happy, you are more photogenic. When you look back at photos where you technically looked good, but you were sad or going through a hard time, you usually won't enjoy looking back at these photos- you may even delete them! On the other hand, photos that you take during happy times with the people you love, or even just the ones by yourself, are memorable and the ones you end up keeping forever!! Even if you didn't originally like how you looked in the photos at the time, over time when you look back you will realize how beautiful you really were and those are the photos you treasure. I have noticed that other people too also usually find the photos where we look or feel the happiest the most attractive! Happiness, warmth and confidence are beautiful.

The photos and videos that capture the true personality of a person are also the most beautiful and attractive. We are not attracted to the 2D physicality of a person, but rather the essence and personality that they convey through their body. A lot of the time we are attracted to someone's behavioral quirks, mannerisms and individual facial expressions.

When you love yourself and are confident in yourself, you will relax more around photos and enjoy yourself more! When you are confident you aren't generally bothered by unflattering photos because you know that that isn't the real you, and also confident people know they are attractive in real life. Life is best lived in the moment and is for enjoying the moment and connecting with people in real life.

If you work in the media or having a screen presence is something very important to you, or if feeling unphotogenic is just something that really gets you down then it is worth remembering that "unphotogenic" is also just a belief created from an early age, and therefore can be changed! We are the Power in our worlds. When we were very small, we internalized messages from the media and the world around us of "not good enough" or "inferior" so that we could be sold expensive beauty products and designer clothes we don't need! Nowadays it's plastic surgery and cosmetic work. These messages of "not good enough" get internalized as low self-esteem and an aspect of this is feeling self-conscious or "not enough" in photos! As you fully love yourself, these negative messages lose power over you. We don't have to continue to buy into someone else's negative beliefs and opinions. Now that we are fully aware of our own Power, we can fully use it for all aspects of our lives! It is time to create a new, positive, empowering beauty reality! Turn any old negativities around with positive statement such as: "I am stunningly, otherworldly gorgeous on camera and 10x even more naturally stunning in real life! The camera captures my gorgeous beauty perfectly." Or: "I love and adore being on camera. I am movie star captivating and my screen presence is mesmerizing." "I love and enjoy taking photos and videos and I feel so confident about myself! I am a fantastic actor/model/presenter/host etc."

-WELLBEING & HEALING-

When you are you at your best; the You-est of You, at one with your Higher Self, your physical body reflects this!! Your skin glows, you are drawn to the right foods and activities for your own vibrant individual essence, your body begins to heal itself and your eyes sparkle. There is a bounce in your step and you walk tall and proud and radiant in who you are!! Even the way you talk, move and walk is beautiful. The high vibration and irresistible magnetism of pure Source Energy when you are connected to your Higher Self channels loving, light, healing radiant energy of Source though your body.

Everybody has unique expressions of their perfect health and wellbeing which is why different diets and exercises work for different people. Some people may feel their most vibrant and alive eating only one meal a day and doing intermittent fasting, whereas other people thrive off 5 small meals a day and eating a breakfast as soon as they wake up! Some people love to lift weights or run whereas other people thrive off doing long walks and yoga. I believe that what we are drawn to and genuinely enjoy, both food and exercise wise, is what benefits our soul and will lead us to the highest expression of our health and wellbeing. The diet and exercise that works best for you is another way of Source expressing itself through the vessel of your body, and by following the right diets, exercise and ways of taking care of your body and mind that work for you, you are honoring and bringing yourself closer to Source! By appreciating and celebrating what works for you individually and following your unique blueprint that Source gave you, you are also showing great respect for yourself and honoring your unique body!

As high vibrations, power and Love of Source radiates through the body, it brings the body back into balance and provides the highest opportunity for the body to heal and align with its Truth. Coming together with your Higher Self is the quickest, easiest and most dependable way to bring your body back into balance, peace and harmony. The love of your True Self, embodied and sustained consistently for a long enough period of time, will harmonize and heal your entire body by bringing high vibrations to the areas that need them- healing energies of Love, Gratitude, Joy and Bliss etc. are so transcendent that they have the ability to transmute and heal any worries and imbalances within the body (David R. Hawkins, *"Healing & Recovery"*). When you are one with Life-Force, your body heals to reflect that same loving, high-vibrational Life-Force energy in accordance to the fullest expression of its own divine blueprint.

A lot of the time, when we are feeling anxious and unsafe in the world, this sense of helplessness or powerlessness reflects in our bodies. What a lot of people experience as health anxiety or body image anxiety is often general anxiety localized, and as the physical body is the closest mirror we have for our relationship with the Universe, it is natural that if we don't feel safe in the Universe our bodies reflect this! Our bodies are the one permanent home we have in the Universe. When we feel safe, secure and loved and cared for by Life, our bodies reflect this sense of peace and safety. The physical body is an external mirror for what is going on inside. When we feel powerful, safe, secure, joyous and ever-safe in Life, our bodies are strong and reflect the joy we feel within ourselves and the Universe.

Healing miracles can and do happen!! If you are in a situation where you need healing, connect with your Higher Power and see what you are naturally guided to do. If you do feel led to work with somebody- including a doctor or a surgeon, then that person has been put in your path by Divine Intelligence. God is in the hands of every surgeon. Connect to your Higher Self and Source first and then see what you are guided to do. Follow your intuition and trust yourself. If you are connected to the Inner You first, then any inspiration or avenues you feel drawn to or naturally comfortable with are in sync with Love.

-TRUE BEAUTY-

I think that at the end of the day, the Truest beauty is high vibrations, positivity and Love. The people who are full of positivity, high vibrations and Love are the most beautiful and the most powerful. David R. Hawkins says in *"Power Vs Force"* that just one person vibrating at the level of 500 (Love) counterbalances 750,000 people vibrating on the levels of 200 (fear) or below.

People who are truly empowered are connected to themselves, love themselves and others and have a radiant effect, transferring their beauty and positivity to the world around them and uplifting others. True beauty is an aspect of Love and therefore like all other aspects of Love, lifts others up to that level and benefits them aswell! Similarly to how being successful from a high vibration also benefits others around you and increases their own success, people who are truly beautiful from a place of authenticity and True Beauty make others feel and become more beautiful.

Even if someone was very physically beautiful but their inside is low-vibrational or insecure, the outside soon matches the inside and they tend to only attract other low-vibrational people long-term. We all have insecurities, but there is difference between having a healthy level of insecurity and having a type of insecurity that has you take it out on others. If you prioritize and over-emphasize physical appearance as an importance, you tend to attract lower-quality, superficial and unhealthy people because people are mirrors to what we hold inside. Therefore, it is always a far better investment of your time to make sure you are working on expressing your True beauty rather than just anything superficial. Outer external appearances are fun and creative expressions of who we are and how we'd like to present ourselves to the world, but they are always one half of a whole- the other half being your Inner Beauty. When you prioritize and lovingly develop both, you will attract healthy, whole and higher-vibrational people who appreciate your inner beauty and are healthy to be around, lifting you up even more and having a positive spiral effect on your life!

Life is a spiritual awakening. Your beauty only increases with experience as you gain more and more wisdom and connect further with the True Self. Beauty comes from within and as you become more and more beautiful on the inside you will only ever become more beautiful and attractive as you move through life. You are a spiritual Being, living in and at one with a supernatural Universe and you are ever-safe in life!

-AFFIRMATIONS FOR BEAUTY-

- I am completely empowered in my body

- I feel very powerful in my body

- I am my own ideal!

- I am exactly how I always wanted to be

- I love and approve of myself

- I love and admire myself

- I am gorgeous, beautiful and perfect inside and out!

- I positively love myself

- I am perfect, gorgeous and I love and approve of myself

- I am my own best friend

- I love how I look and feel in myself

- There is no one I'd rather be

- I am my own hero/my own idol

- I am my own epitome of perfection

- I love being me!

- I feel very powerful in myself

Positive Affirmations

- I can do anything

- I love being able to do all the activities I want to do (*sports/physical activities*)

- I love and relish being in my body

- My body is amazing and capable of incredible things

- I love and approve of my perfect body

- My body is my best friend

- I feel ever-safe in the Universe

- I feel completely safe in my body

- My body is gorgeous, perfect and incredible

- I feel unbelievably confident!

- I am delighted with myself

- I feel so good about myself

- I am the fullest, highest, most beautiful version of me!

- I love and appreciate the unique gift of who I am!

- I love, honor and respect myself!

- I am radiant and perfect

- I love and admire myself. I am True Beauty

- I uplift everyone around me

-BEAUTY AND SELF-CONFIDENCE-

- I am unique, special and wonderful

- I have a special kind of beauty. Everyone on the planet has their own unique, special brand of beauty. I love, celebrate and admire my own unique, gorgeous beauty

- I am radiant and attractive

- I love, honor and approve of myself. I treat myself with love and respect

- I honor my unique body and what works for me. I treasure the foods that work best with my body and relish in taking exercise that my body loves

- I love, approve of and believe in myself

- I am the most beautiful person in my Universe

- I am the most beautiful person to my soulmate/soul people/soul friends/soul family

- I am wonderful and I love everything about me that makes me unique and stand out

- I understand that everybody has their own idea of beautiful. Beauty is in the eye of the beholder. Everybody has different eyes

- I love and delight in being me!

- It is so much fun being me

Positive Affirmations

- I love the way I look and feel! I adore myself and I find myself so attractive. I love myself and I am gorgeous

- I love life and Life loves me. I am happy to be alive!

- Every day it is a joy to wake up with the gift of being myself

- I am a unique, precious gift

- Every day with myself is a blessing

- Every day as myself is a joy and a gift.

- I am so proud to be me.

- There is no else like me

- I am glowing and gorgeous

- Every day I just become more and more supernaturally attractive and otherworldly beautiful

- I live in a miraculous, supernatural Universe and I am one with an otherworldly Power

- I am one with Life-Force. I am ever-safe in the Universe. Life loves me

- I am exquisitely, dazzlingly gorgeous

- I am grateful and delighted for my supernatural, gorgeous attractive aura

- My body is always on my side. I love and trust my body

-BEAUTY AND SELF-CONFIDENCE-

- I love and trust my amazing body. My body is always there for me!!

- Every day I just become more and more supernaturally fit, supernaturally attractive, dazzlingly healthy and gorgeous

- I have a unique, dazzlingly gorgeous, glowing beautiful Aura

- The beauty of my soul is radiant, transcendent, iridescent and irresistible

- I have a dazzling, irresistibly beautiful mind

- I have a brave, beautiful heart and soul

- I have a unique fire spirit and a beautiful, mesmerizing deep soul

- I am unearthly gorgeous, mesmerizing and primal.

- I am in touch with the Earth and connected to Nature. I love and approve of myself wherever I go

- I am supported by the Earth. I am deeply rooted here

- I am gorgeous and glowing. I radiate pure Love and Fire wherever I go

- I feel so complete within myself. I am completely full by myself.

- My body/self is a constant source of pleasure and delight

- I am so thankful for the gift of myself! Thank you Life. I am one with Life. I am at one with the Universe.

10.

-DREAM LIFE VIBRATION -

AFFIRMATIONS FOR DREAM LIFE

This is another short set of affirmations, this time designed around the vibration of your dream life. This set of affirmations is written from the point of you already being in your dream life. You are there already!

Everybody has different dreams. Some desire to be rich, famous and celebrated whereas others want nothing more than a quiet and idyllic, peaceful life; humble and down to Earth. Whatever it is that we want externally, the only reason we want it is because we believe it will make us happy inside.

Feel happy first, and as you attune your vibration to the frequency of happiness, everything that you desire will be drawn unto you.

I also believe this works visa versa- focusing on your goals and feeling the fulfillment of your desires generates happy feelings, which then draws your dreams and more happiness to you! If you sincerely feel happy and fulfilled thinking about your dreams, then they vibrate the essence of Love and Fulfillment out from you.

This draws all kinds of widespread happiness on the frequency to you. I also believe that our deepest desires and dreams of our heart are beneficial to dwell on, because they carry the vibration of our heart. When we dwell on and allow ourselves to enjoy the feelings of our wishes being fulfilled, we are attuning to our heart vibration, our dharma and destiny.

As dreams are all so highly individual, I have just written a brief outline of how a dream life can feel. Like all the other chapters before, you can re-arrange and use these affirmations for your liking, to tailor them to your own unique individual dreams and desires. The key essential is that you feel the essence of excitement, deep fulfillment, joy and your own personal Heaven on Earth! When you live your dream life, the overall feeling is one of deep joy, wondrous fulfillment, excitement, peace, bliss, satisfaction, radiance, Power and Oneness and deep gratitude for the Universe. You feel alive, loving, thriving and complete. It is pure Heaven on Earth!

-DREAM LIFE AFFIRMATIONS-

- I am an international, abundantly successful, outrageously complete Multi-Millionaire, happy and fulfilled and loved. I have everything I ever want or need. It is pure Heaven on Earth.

- I am an international, famous, ridiculously successful Multi-Millionaire in my dream field/industry, 100% fulfilled and complete living the life of my dreams

- I am living pure Heaven on Earth

- I am living the life I always wanted

- I have everything I could ever want or need

- Life loves me.

- The Universe blesses me

- The Universe loves me. Life abundantly supports me.

- Life is always there for me

- I am endlessly supported and held by the Universe.

- I am cocooned in a sea of infinite prosperity, bliss and love

- I am surrounded by love wherever I go. Love is within me, all around me and flows through me endlessly.

- I live joyfully and at peace, with abundance in the life of my dreams

- I live joyfully, luxuriously and safely in the house/home of my dreams that always profits me

- I live in the exact dream location I always want to live in, with the perfect people and one with the Universe

- I am happy, free, blissful, peaceful and one with All of Life

- I live blissfully, peacefully and abundantly fulfilled with my true divine soulmate, my love of dreams

- I am now together with the love of my life!

- I have the relationship from Heaven, my love of dreams. It is beyond perfect

- My relationship is from Heaven. It is so exciting, deeply, deeply fulfilling, what I always wanted and everything I ever asked for and more. I am in awe and deep gratitude for the Universe. Every day I am giddy with gratitude and joy and grateful for my love

- I am so lucky to be with my true divine soulmate love, now and forever

- I feel so relaxed, safe, secure, beautiful/handsome, confident and at ease with my soulmate. They are deeply exciting, fulfilling, thrilling and leave me breathless/walking on air/weak at the knees at the same.

Positive Affirmations

- The relationship Flows. It's so easy. The Universe does all the work. I am safe with my soulmate and the Universe, now and forever.

- Life truly is Bliss. I am so happy. Every day I wake up overwhelmed with Love & Gratitude. Love courses through my veins and radiates out to everyone I meet. I am pure Love and Light.

- Every day just gets better and better for me. I am at one with the Universe

- Life loves me and wants only Good for me. I am one with the Power that created the Universe and woke me up [spiritual awakening that made you aware of law of attraction/The Universe]

- All and only Good fills my life now.

- My life is a living Paradise, a true Heaven on Earth.

- I am always safe in life.

- I trust the Universe.

- Life loves me, and I love life!

-DREAM LIFE VIBRATION -

-EPILOGUE-

 emember that your life can be unlimited good. <u>There is no end to the Paradise we can create.</u> Positivity has no limits.

This doesn't mean there won't ever be challenges, unexpected events or human rites of passage such as Death etc., but it's how we deal with them that counts. When we change our perceptions and attitudes towards a situation, the energy around that situation changes. When you change the way you look at things, the things you look at change.

When we handle a situation with Love, gratitude, acceptance and a willingness to learn and grow from the situation, we bring light to the situation and transform it. Even the most upsetting events like death or a serious health challenge can deepen one's heart and open you up to more and deeper Love.

When you remember your loved one with joy, gratitude and appreciation for all the time you had together and that they were in your life in the first place, and accept that grief and missing them means that you deeply loved them, the sadness and pain in a way becomes a celebration and a reminder of that deep love! It also helps to remember that your loved one never really leaves you. I believe in life after death, and that our loved ones go to Heaven; a realm of dimension that is pure Source Energy, formless yet form at the same time, always changing, renewing, breaking down and transforming for the sheer joy of it! Life loves creation, change and transition. I think that when we die we return to the Source dimension where we came from, and then when we want to choose a new experience we can reincarnate into a new body! The new body we choose won't always necessarily be human. We may choose to come back as a star, a tree, a plant, a flower, a rock or an animal for a lifetime. I also believe that because God/Source Energy/the Universe is omnipotent and omniscient, our loved ones can simultaneously reside in the Heaven dimension watching over us and they can also choose to be with us at the same time, hence why sometimes you will feel them with you, see signs, hear their voices, see them in a 'dream', for example. I don't think people choose to go into a new incarnation till everyone they love and have a connection with on Earth has passed over themselves, unless they want to come back in a different form to their loved one during that lifetime. If they do stay in Heaven till we have all also passed, I believe everyone then decides what they'll do next together and how they'll meet and be with each other again in the next life!

We can add Positivity to any situation. Even in the darkest situations we can choose to shine a Light. When we become light, we transform the darkness around us. This especially works on a collective level- the more light and positivity each of us shines, the more light we vibrate out into the planet! It isn't selfish to shine your light- it is the complete opposite. It is selfless, giving and helpful to others to make yourself as happy as possible and to become as empowered as you can in all areas of your life. When we are empowered in ourselves, we are Powerful- so Powerful that we co-create and contribute to a more light-filled, loving, harmonious world.

A great source of inspiration is watching people who didn't have the best start, multiple failures, challenges in life, obstacles and setbacks etc., and watching how they gracefully dealt with their challenges and used them to create even more love and add more meaning to their lives. A friend once told me she finds it fascinating to see how different people handle a situation. As Louise Hay says, some of us have a few challenges, others have a lot. Wherever we are and wherever we start from, we all come from Love and I believe Life is a journey of awakening to the Divine Love within you and embodying more and more of that Love until we transition on!

When you give out love, you get love back. When you give out positivity, you receive positivity back. When you give out Good, you will receive Good back to you. It *is* that simple.

If you enjoyed these affirmations, I have another book written later called: *"Paradise is a State of Mind; Affirmations for Love, Bliss and Dreams."* A lot of this second book is similar to this one, but I expanded upon it in some places and cut back on it in others. Basically, the tone is different. I wrote *Paradise* based on my highest-vibrational experiences whereas this book is more grounded and good to read if you are going through challenges.

You can also check out the main people/further reading who influenced me most. You will find them on the *Acknowledgements* page following.

Thank you for reading this book. I hope there was at least one thing in it that helped you in some way.

Have an amazing day!

-ACKNOWLEDGEMENTS-

There have been a lot of different people who have influenced this short book and each one has added something unique, special and valuable along the journey. I believe our Soul is on a journey of awakening and draws you to specific books, mentors and resources at specific times so you can learn something from that person and move on. No teacher is our guru- our own Soul is- but each teacher gives you a unique precious gift. It can be just one nugget of knowledge or wisdom, but that one nugget could change your life and evolve you to your next level on your journey. These gems of information and transformation all integrate within our being and work together like a beautiful tapestry to create you into more of who you Are.

-ACKNOWLEDGEMENTS-

Principal influences in writing this book:

Louise Hay is my principal influence, she has a way of making you feel Heaven on Earth and Paradise. Whenever I read or listen to Louise Hay, I feel fulfilled and like I already have everything I need, although optimistic for the good that is coming at the same time. Louise Hay changed my life.

Julia Rogers Hamrick of the *Easy World* series is my second most significant influence. Her *Easy World* books currently are not so well-known, but to me her frequency, energy and knowledge is beyond most well-known spiritual teachers today. Her precipice is that joy, love and high vibrations are the only thing we need and that life is meant to be easy! It is also based on the love of a Higher Power.

David R. Hawkins was another strong influence in my life. Although I don't read his work much now, his work on the vibrational scale solidified what I- and I know many of us- have learnt through life & experience – that Love, Joy & Gratitude is the answer. His chapter on the Vibrational Power and nature of Love is excellent.

Tuesday May Thomas is another relatively under-the-radar teacher and her book *"Manifesting with the Law of Vibration"* is again Paradisiacal vibrations. It is about trusting the Truth of your heart and a Higher Power to guide your life rather than your mind and ego- because the heart is Infinite Intelligence that knows you better than you know yourself, and knows what will make you 100% happy (and it wants this for you). Often we try to choose and focus on goals with our minds because we are certain of what we need to make us happy, but the heart has eyes of its own and can see to a deeper level exactly what we need to fulfill us on every level. Think of the times when you got what you asked for, but even better with things you hadn't have even thought to ask, or the times you didn't get what you wanted but only because something better was waiting for you. The heart knows.

I encourage you to check out any of these teachers above; ultimately your journey is *yours* and whatever you do, your own Soul will always lead you to your own perfect resources at the right time regardless.

ABOUT THE AUTHOR

Alexia Eden has a BSc degree in Biomedical Sciences and has worked in the financial services industry in London and in the hospitality and nightlife industries in Ibiza and Barcelona. She has worked various acting jobs in England and Spain. She loves travelling, languages, animals and electronic/techno music. She is qualified to instruct yoga and to practise Usui reiki @alexia.eden

Printed in Great Britain
by Amazon

26567701R00066